HOW TO SURVIVE
WITH SPROUTING

D1566953

How to SURVIVE with SPROUTING

by

BRUFORD SCOTT REYNOLDS

Recipes
Collected and Tested
by
Dorothy K. Reynolds

Sprouts Grown
by
James Alan Reynolds

Illustrations
by
John Marlin Reynolds

Published by

HAWKES PUBLISHING, INC.
156 W. 2170 S. (P.O. Box 15711)
Salt Lake City, Utah 84115
phone: 487-1695
or toll free: (800) 453-4616

ISBN 0-89036-028-6

Originally Published by
The Reynolds Enterprise

First Edition
March 1970

Copyright 1973
by Hawkes Publishing, Inc.

Enlarged Edition
with Illustrations and Index

TYPESETTING

BY

HAWKES PUBLISHING, INC.

MAGAZINE PRINTING and PUBLISHING

Printing
and
Binding
by

2255 SOUTH WEST TEMPLE
SALT LAKE CITY, UTAH 84115
PHONE (801) 486-2351

Printed in U.S.A.

FOREWORD

Due to so many requests from people interested in becoming health-minded, wanting to live longer, wanting to save money on food and wanting to do their own sprouting, we have written this book.

We hope it will encourage them and help them to achieve their desires.

In this book we make no promise that you will live to the age of a tree — but — we do say that if you will become more health conscious and teach your children to be the same, you will enjoy a longer, more productive life, and your children will definitely benefit.

Sprouting is not only a good means of providing more natural vitamins and minerals, it is easy to do and also inexpensive. See what we've got to say about it, and happy eating!

Bruford Scott Reynolds

TABLE OF CONTENTS

Page:

Section I

GROWING SPROUTS

THANK YOU, EVERYONE

We wish to thank the many people who have helped bring about health ideas and thus inspired us on to do something with sprouts.

And a special thanks to all who helped with the information and the recipes in this book.

The aim of this book is to improve our present eating habits by taking well-liked recipes and improving the nutritional value of each recipe by substituting sprouted foods in place of energy-robbing, refined-dead foods. In this we have not sacrificed eye appeal or flavor. The one big thing we did do was to add large amounts of vitamins and minerals to the recipes with the use of sprouts.

VALUES

Few people know very much about sprouts or their food value. The one thing they do know is that when seeds are planted and given the right amounts of warmth, moisture, and fresh air, it is almost impossible to stop them from sprouting. It is a God-given principle for all things that they should multiply and fill the earth.

For some reason which we mere mortals can only guess, sprouts at this time have more life-giving acids and vitamins than at any other time in the plant's life.

So — why not use this high vitamin and amino acid content when it is at its best?

Sprouts, when they start to turn green, are rich with chlorophyll, which is very important in the building of your body. Chlorophyll is the life blood of plants and it is similar to human blood. Only a few atoms of chemicals keep it from being perfect blood.

PROOF OF THE PUDDING ... IS IN THE EATING

All the recipes in this book have been tried and tested by various individuals in actual family situations. Some of our neighbors and friends have also tried many of the recipes and they again passed the eating test. So you may try them with delight.

The knowledge contained in this book could very well help in times of hardship and stress; when we may have to be "Sprouting" to survive. It is only good sense to acquaint our families with this type of eating now instead of waiting for it to be forced upon us.

Let us reap the rewards of the good health that it will bring now. Let us not wait. Tomorrow may be too late. Start eating large amounts of SPROUTED SALADS — TODAY — and EVERY DAY.

SPROUTS AND POISONS

One of the great advantages of eating sprouts is that it only takes three to five days to sprout most seeds to eating size. In this short time the sprouts have not had time to become infected with insects; therefore, they have not had to be sprayed with poison.

When you eat sprouts, you eat pure, live, fresh food from the garden; untouched by any killer of man or insect.

If you plan to raise your own sprouts, be sure that you use pure water; when we say PURE WATER, we mean just that. Do not use water that has been through the "WATER SOFTENER," water that has CHLORINE in it, or FLUORIDE water. In some big cities, this will be a little difficult; but plants just do not like water additives that kill. You can raise plants in water instead of soil (Hydroponics) by the adding of proper mineral nutrients to the water; these solutions are food for the plant. You do not need to add solutions to your sprout's water. The food for the sprout is in the seed; when this is all used up, the sprouts become a plant and as such must then have food placed in the water, but not until then. In fact, you can grow your sprouts in distilled water.

Sprouts grown in your own home from good seeds are the safest food in America today.

Be sure the seeds you buy are untreated and fresh. Buy them by the pound and cut your food bill in half.

Save even more—buy them by the one hundred pounds.

HUNGER DISEASE

Have you ever gone to a Chinese Restaurant and eaten your fill of steamed fresh foods, then one hour later been so hungry that you felt you had not eaten? You have heard of many that have had this feeling. This is the result of years of wrong eating habits that come from eating over-cooked foods. Over-cooking takes out the vitamins, water, live enzymes and minerals leaving behind a pile of dead waste material that has to be flavored and doctored with all kinds of salts, spices, and herbs to make it palatable.

When you change your diet to a fresh, live-food diet, you will notice the hunger disease coming on; do not let

— IT — get you. It takes time to overcome the habit of eating dead waste.

Many have already started — why not you? START TODAY! — You will save money.

You will notice in our cook booklet that we have included many meals which include meats of all kinds, cooked fruits and vegetables. Eat sparingly of cooked meats and fill up on sprouts. Soon you will leave all meat alone and start enjoying fresh, live foods.

If you like them warm or hot, follow some of the recipes but be sure that you DO NOT OVER-COOK any of the fresh vegetables or sprouts. You always add the sprouts just before serving.

Some people are allergic to certain fresh foods; therefore, steaming or cooking them may kill the product in the food causing the trouble. For example, people who are allergic to Vitamin "C" must remember that Soybean sprouts have about eight times the "C" content of oranges or lemons, so if you cannot eat oranges or lemons, you may still be able to eat Soybeans but — be cautious about it, until you are sure.

Remember food for one person may be poison for another. You are the only one who knows what is best for you. If you don't, the test is simple. Eat your fill of one type of food; if it upsets your system or causes you to have the symptoms of a common cold, cross it off your list. If you like it, eat it sparingly — never overeat anything. You may not know it, but a mild case of food poisoning has the same symptoms as a common cold. In fact, nearly half of all the common colds are not colds but mild cases of food poisoning. That is why it is best to eat fresh vegetables, sprouts and fruit. Treatment is the same as for the common cold. Drink extra amounts of — water — wash that phony cold or poison out of your system and be sure you eat food rich in Vitamin C.

KING OF SPROUTS

Many people have called Alfalfa the "King of Sprouts."

LET'S SEE WHY:

Many centuries ago, the Arabs fed their horses Alfalfa to make them strong and fast. After finding what it would do for their horses, they ate it themselves and found that they could run great distances and broad-jump well over 25 feet.

The Arabs were probably the first to experiment with this plant and because of its life-giving properties they gave it its name "AL-FAL-FA" which to them meant: "Father of All Foods."

As Alfalfa became more known, it spread to Persia and then it was introduced into Greece about 480 B.C.: from there to Italy in the first century, and from Italy it spread slowly over Europe and was carried by the Spaniards to Mexico in the sixteenth century, where it soon spread north and south.

Alfalfa has been known for hundreds of years as one of the best foods for livestock, and not until now have our men of science come up with facts the Arabs knew centuries before Christ.

The Arabs did not have the fancy names or vitamin names that we have now. They just knew that Alfalfa was good for man and beast.

SCIENTIFIC FINDINGS

Our scientific researchers have discovered that Alfalfa contains at least eight essential enzymes required in the digestion of foods. It also contains all kinds of cell-building amino acids so important in a healthful body.

Some of these acids are: Arginine, Lysine, Theronine, and Triptophane.

They have also found it contains all known Vitamins including Vitamin K, the blood-clotting vitamin, that is so necessary in healing of cuts.

A two ounce cup of Alfalfa seeds—soaked overnight, then placed in a 2-inch by 9-inch by 12-inch tray and watered according to instructions—will yield this tray full of fresh delicious Alfalfa Sprouts.

They found it very rich in minerals such as:

Potassium — this is very important in keeping young and agile.

Phosphorus — which speeds up brain vibrations, and is called by so many, "The Elixir of Life."

Calcium — for the bones and the teeth.

Magnesium, Sodium silicon, and many more.

One of the other valuable properties of Alfalfa is the great amount of Chlorophyll it contains. Chlorophyll is very good for its photosynthesis and powerful oxidation catalyst.

Alfalfa has been known for a long time as a skin conditioner. It has been used to clear the eyes and to help correct arthritic conditions. It has also been used to clear up acne conditions.

YOU ARE WHAT YOU EAT

It has been proven that the chlorophyll, enzymes, minerals and vitamins found in Alfalfa serve as an aid in digestion and stimulate lagging appetites.

Some of the Enzymes found in Alfalfa are:

Lipase—a fat-splitting enzyme,

Amylase—which acts upon starch,

Coagulase—to coagulate blood,

Emulsin—that acts upon sugar,

Invertase—which converts cane sugar into dextrose,

Peroxidase—which has an oxidizing effect on the blood,

Pectinase—an enzyme that forms a vegetable jelly from a pectin substance,

Protase—which digests proteins.

There are 22 enzymes essential to the body. Some of these the body makes itself when it cannot get them some place else.

Along with all the other qualities of Alfalfa, it contains a little-known vitamin which has proven to be of great help in the healing of peptic ulcers. In fact, according to the records, 80 percent so treated were healed. This little-known vitamin is Vitamin U.

For more information, read the works of Dr. Garnett of the Stanford University, in California.

It also has been reported that Alfalfa has been used as a rebuilder of decayed teeth, not just a decay-preventative agent.

For more information, read the books on life-saving plants and grasses. One very good book is:

Nature's Healing Grasses, by H. C. Kirschner, M.D.

There are many good books on proper eating and the use of good food. Why not visit your health food store or your bookstore?

THE STAFF OF LIFE—WHEAT

There are many, many books written about wheat and wheat products and why it is called "The Staff of Life."

Never does a day go by that you do not call upon wheat to perform some duty. Just a few examples, to give you an idea:

Paste—to hold your wallpaper; paste for children to use that is non-poisonous.

Paper Products—and many paper paste items, Papier-mache ornaments.

Binders—in tablets and pills to hold the medicine the doctors want you to take.

Binder—in making rabbit and other animal pellets for feed, such as Alfalfa and grain pellets.

The list is so long that by the time we get to something to eat we have filled a book. So let us stop here and get to the eating of wheat.

Wheat, in itself, dry, is chiefly starch and carbohydrates with very few vitamins. One end has what is called a wheat germ that has a good number of Vitamin B's (chiefly Vitamin B-1), nothing outstanding.

Now, suppose you could take that little wheat germ and make it give you everlasting life? Suppose you could by some little trick make that germ give you a fountain of youth? Suppose you could make that little wheat germ cure all your colds, cancers, asthmas, nervousness, and food worries? Suppose by the proper use of this germ and some of the other seed sprouts known as pulse or herbs, you could cut your food bill in half and then in half again and be more healthy?

Oh — I must be dreaming; nothing could do that! I must have had too many glasses of milk before I wrote that. And yet the Scriptures contain these words, recorded for all to read:

> All grain is good for the food of man; as also the fruit of the vine; that which yieldeth fruit, whether in the ground or above the ground.
>
> Nevertheless, wheat for man, and corn for the ox, and oats for the horse, and rye for the fowls and for swine, and for all beasts of the field, and barley for all useful animals, and for mild drinks, as also other grains.
>
> ...Every herb in the season thereof, and every fruit in the season thereof; all these to be used with prudence and thanksgiving.

In other verses, a promise is given that all who follow this counsel will be healthy and have a long life. It also states that one may run and not be weary and shall walk and not faint. And I do not doubt these words one little bit.

You know and your neighbors know and your doctors know that wheat is fattening; it is full of carbohydrates and starch even when toasted. If you want to lose weight, leave bread alone and by all means all cookies, cakes, and gravy. In fact, anything made of wheat, for they are all NO-NO'S!

Someone must be off their rocker. So let us see what we can do about it. First, let us say, we know all about wheat as wheat which is ground into flour and goes into bread and other fattening eatables.

O.K.

So, to find out more, we have to do something, make tests, play games, experiment, and live a little. First go to your hay, grain and feed store, or if you are so inclined, go to the health food store. On second thought, go to your health food store. They will not laugh over what I want you to do, for they are probably already doing it.

Ask for a pound of clean, untreated wheat. You know, the kind that will grow; the kind where the wheat germ is still alive. Tell them, "I want to plant it and make it grow." Well, a good health nut knows exactly what you are going to do and you have a friend and if you can get out of the store without buying two or three books on better living, you will do more than I did.

Second, hurry right home and find an old box or nail some old boards together about the size of a tomato or fruit lug. Any size around 14 inches wide by 24 inches long; about 4 inches deep. The wheat does not care as long as you don't, so just do it.

Third, if you have too many holes in the box, put an old piece of nylon stocking over the holes. If the holes are too big, put a piece of wire screen or heavy cloth over it.

Fourth, place one inch of clean sand on the bottom of the box; then cover this with some real good soil with compost mixed in it.

Fifth, spread a layer of wheat over this soil and then a little soil on top of the wheat. (If you want your wheat to sprout faster, soak it in warm water overnight. Not hot water, you do not want to cook it).

Sixth, keep your wheat field in a warm place, not in direct sunlight. Why not in sunlight? Because the blades of grass will absorb too much chlorophyll from the sun and will have a strong taste. On second thought, maybe you will like the strong taste—I don't. That strong taste is good for you. You should have it.

Seventh, keep your garden damp, warm, and with plenty of light and nothing will stop it from growing. In the winter, hang a 100 watt bulb over it.

Eighth, when your garden is about 4 to 6 inches tall, it is ready for eating. Cut about 4 ounces off one side. Do not cut it all the way down. Let it grow up again like grass. Cut a little each day.

Ninth, Now eat it. What? Well eat it. That is what I said, EAT IT. "How?" In many ways. Just take some and put it in your mouth and chew it until all that green stuff is out. You know, that Chlorophyll and those hundreds of units of vitamins and minerals never heard of in wheat before. Now spit the waste string out and go for another handful. You will not get more health-building enzymes, vitamins, or minerals any place else. If this doesn't please you, try cutting the grass in one-half inch lengths and mixing them with your salad or sprinkle them on a thin slice of bread in place of lettuce. Mix them with a scrambled egg. O.K., so you do not like that. Take about 4 ounces and put them in your blender or juicer, add enough water to make eight ounces of drink. Let the blender run to get the juice all out and then press the grass strings out. This drink has a kick to it. It makes my stomach do a twitch. I either thin it down with more water or add some fruit juice to it.

Always use the wheat juice fresh from your garden—the longer it stands unused, the more value is lost.

With good care and proper watering, adding a little compost once in a while, this pound of wheat could last you all year. The wheat eats up the soil fast. Be sure your planter is deep enough.

Let us look at it this way: You go into partnership with Mother Nature and you chip in the first 25 cents and the box. She will furnish the sunlight and dirt. You keep the mix wet and you can eat a big green salad every day. Worth trying, don't you think so? You will live longer; it might be for only one day, but a day is a day and someday a doctor may discover something that will increase your life for years. It could be just what you are going to try. So let's get started. How is your one year's supply of wheat? I mean your growing wheat, not your dead wheat used for flour.

If you are not very handy with nails and a hammer, get some large flower pots. Even some old plastic egg cartons work wonders as planters for wheat.

Well, here is a toast to better health. A green water toast. WOW! Anything that strong is bound to be good for you. Where's the fruit juice? Good luck—and I hope you live to be 200.

Did you know that before World War II, a few Universities were experimenting making flour out of wheat grass? It had a good taste, kind of a nut flavor, with a cream color and all kinds of minerals and vitamins. It surely seems a waste of good food, time and money and a great loss to man's food supply that they stopped working on it.

SPROUTED WHEAT

There is a big difference between eating dry wheat or wheat products, and eating sprouted wheat or slow-dried sprouted wheat and wheat grass.

The big difference being that dry wheat is chiefly made of carbohydrates, starch, proteins and if the wheat germ has not been removed, Vitamin B's.

When you sprout wheat for three days, you add to the wheat: **enzymes, amino acids, more vitamins,** and **minerals.**

Now let the wheat grow 10 days and you add **chlorophyll.** You will lose some of the benefits of the fresh sprouts but you gain chlorophyll.

The two very best plants for chlorophyll are the wheat grasses and alfalfa. These two plants together make a green drink that cannot be equaled.

So it depends upon what you want. Eat accordingly, and sprout accordingly.

Sprouts for all wheat sprout recipes should be sprouted until the sprout is no longer than the wheat itself. Exceptions are:

All bread recipes, the recipes where flour is also used, which call for sprouts that are sprouted ½ the length of the kernel itself—if they are any longer, the bread will be sticky.

For drinks or a strictly health soup where added chlorophyll is desired, you should sprout the wheat additional lengths and expose them to light, (sun or artificial), for the greening process. Wheat grass is grown about 6 inches long for salads and for Green Manna drinks.

To improve a salad, vitamin and chlorophyll wise— add ½ cup of wheat grass cut into ¼ or ½ inch lengths and mix them into your recipes.

If you want to save money and improve your health — DO IT.

AFTER THOUGHT

Be careful — I read someplace where they were experimenting with Alfalfa sprouts on some old horses and cows. After a few months on this diet, the horses went out and had colts and the old cows had calves. Remember Sarah in the Bible had a child in her old age. Maybe she changed her diet to sprouts. Now — do not get carried away. It is just a thought.

ANOTHER THOUGHT:

It was told to us that a young mother should eat Alfalfa sprouts and drink Alfalfa tea. We know of one young mother who had trouble nursing her new babies. She tried this with her latest child; now she has plenty of milk and the baby is doing great. No costly formulas as before. Not only is the baby content, but all of the family including daddy is happy over the new found peace that it brings to the house.

ANOTHER THOUGHT:

Someplace I read that the day would come that man would live to the age of a tree; and the Lion would lay down with the Lamb. What would they eat? Why grasses of the field, of course. We might as well get started NOW.

ISAIAH 11:7

"and the Lion shall eat straw like the ox."

SOYBEANS

The Soybean is a close relative to the Mung Bean and is used in many of the same ways. There are many outstanding points in the favor of the Soybean, but they are harder to sprout. One of the outstanding points is that the Vitamin C content is the highest.

If you live in an area where it is hard to get Vitamin C, sprout some Soybeans. One-half cup full is equal to six glasses of orange juice.

The Soybeans, like all the other beans, have practically no Vitamin count in the dry stage. Yet, sprouted for three days, the Vitamin C count jumps up to around 700 milligrams and the Vitamin B complexes also jump up. B-1, Niacin and Pantothenic acid double. Biotin and Pyridoxine increase 150 percent. Vitamin B-2 and Folic acid jump up to a 500 percent increase.

Most beans are an excellent and cheap source of food energy and a valuable source of vegetable protein. They may be used as a suitable substitute for muscle meat.

Most beans are outstanding sources of Vitamin B and are good for helping to stimulate the appetite and to keep the nerves healthy. Most beans are excellent sources of minerals.

Soybeans have been used to replace all the products of the cow: meat, butter, cheese and milk.

—SOYBEAN CHART—

Information taken from the USDA Handbook No. 80
"Composition of Foods"

	Dry	Sprouted
Protein	38	48
Fat	20	14
Carbohydrate	38	37
Vitamin A	90 IU	800 IU
Thiamine B	1.2	1.6
Riboflavin B	0.35	1.5
Niacin B	2.4	7.0
Ascorbic Acid (Vitamin C)	0	100

In percent or grams per 100 grams of dry weight.

While the above information is for Soybeans, similar results might reasonably be expected from other sprouted seeds.

SPROUTING RULES

The rules to follow are: most sprouts are grown in the dark. This gives them a white, clear appearance and a mild, nut flavor. However, if you wish them to have chlorophyll added, you must expose them to light. The darker green they become, the more chlorophyll they contain. Some people do not like the strong taste of dark green chlorophyll even though it is good for you. In some sprouts, such as beans, do not try for chlorophyll. You may lose your garden before the green comes and you might get an odor which is not pleasing.

For different beans, use different sprouting times and methods.

FOR EXAMPLE:

Pinto Beans:

Fill a two-quart pan with water and soak one pint of beans 12 hours to expand. This starts the bean to grow and it builds up a supply of reserve water which the sprout uses as it develops. After 12 hours, spread beans out on a tray that has a towel or several sheets of cotton cloth on the bottom. Be sure to rinse beans every 4 or 5 hours, then drain. "AGAIN," do not sprout over 3 days. If the sprouts are more than one-fourth inch long, the beans may become mushy and stink.

Soybeans:

Soybeans must have several changes of water, at least 3 or 4 times while soaking them in their 12-hour swelling period. Why? It seems that Soybeans have an anti-digestant enzyme in them and it must be leached out. You will find that other beans will do better if you change their water two or three times also. No seed likes stale water. However, this is only important when sprouting beans of the Soybean family.

Mung Beans:

Mung Beans are best when sprouted 2 or 3 inches long. Be sure of your seed. ASK — "ARE THEY FRESH?"

Some beans will not sprout to three inches in length. This does not take away the food value. In fact, some say to not sprout them more than one inch or you start to lose the vitamins. If you ask me how I like them, it is ½ inch on up, as long as they are crisp and solid like celery. I eat them by the handful right from the trays. Mung Beans should be used as soon as you take them from the tray and should be eaten raw for the most vitamins. They do not keep very well in the refrigerator—3 or 4 days, a week at the most. Do not use them after they turn brown and go soft. Throw them away.

For other beans, sprout as you would Pinto Beans. Personally, I change the water a couple of times even though it is not necessary on Pinto, Red, Navy, Lentil,

Lima, Blackeye, or Kidney. I do not like to see the water bubble and turn colors. It reminds me of the smell of beer and if you let it stand too long, it stinks! Some of the health addicts say to keep it because it is full of minerals and makes good soup.

O.K.—So it makes good soup; you try it, I don't want to.

Alfalfa:

When you sprout Alfalfa, soak the seeds around 12 hours and you can let them grow 5 or even 6 days depending upon how much chlorophyll you want. Remember — after 4 days sprouts start to become plants and will have a stronger taste and odor. The older it gets, the stronger it gets. Some people like it. But remember — the older it gets, the less Vitamin E you get, along with the losing of other vitamins.

Now, do you want vitamins or chlorophyll? O.K. So raise two trays and mix the six-day old with the three-day old and get both. That should make you happy.

Alfalfa sprouts hold up very well in the refrigerator. We kept some as long as one month just to see how they would keep; they were still crisp and tasty after that length of time.

Alfalfa sprouts, like most babies, like nice, warm places to grow. Keep the room around 80 degrees. Do not go below 55 or the cold will retard the growth and you will get a sickly plant. If the room gets over 80, you must water the sprouts more often, because the plants grow faster with heat and absorb more air and water to fill out the new cells. If you don't give them the water they need, they will dry out and turn brown. So for your best results, keep them at room temperature during the day (about 80 degrees) and at night around 60, then you will not have to worry about watering them while you sleep.

Onions or Spice Sprouts:

For sprouts such as onions, garlic, parsley, and others, where you want the green tops rather than the seed sprouts, let them grow up to ten days or longer. You can then juice them or cut them into one-fourth inch pieces and sprinkle on salads or in soups or casseroles. They are great. Radish is hot — somewhat like garlic. Take it easy until you know how strong you want them. Remember, a radish will reach its full size under ideal conditions in 28 days, so do not sprout them too long or you will not have sprouts, just store-bought radish.

Parsley:

Parsley you can let grow and put in a flower pot. Cut a little everytime you want some flavoring. It will grow

back if you give it proper care. They tell me it is a
wonderful nerve tonic made into a tea drink. Dry some
and try it. It has lots of vitamins, high in C and E, the
youth vitamin. For only a 10 or 15 cent package of seeds,
you can have parsley flavoring all year long if you take
care of it.

Grow them in a sun-lighted window box or flower
pot. If you have the space outside, plant them and keep
cutting them down, drying the tops for winter use.

THE TEN DO NOT'S

1. Do not leave seeds in water over 20 hours or under
   10; 12 hours is best.
2. Do not let seeds set in water while sprouting. They
   will drown and sour. Be sure they drain well.
3. Do not use chemically treated city water. Chlorine
   will kill the sprouts.
4. Do not use HOT water or COLD water. Hot water
   will cook them — cold water will retard the growth.
   Keep between 50 and 80 degrees.
5. Do not sprout over 4 days. Sprouts then become
   plants. A sprout is when a seed begins to grow, then
   it becomes a plant, then whatever God intended it to
   be, be it grass or a tree.

6. Do not let the seeds or sprouts dry out. Water them morning and night and 2 or 3 times a day. The sprouts will turn brown if they dry out.

7. Do not buy cheap seeds or old, hard seeds. They take a longer soaking period to bring them to life. They may already be dead and will not sprout.

8. Do not buy treated seeds that have been poisoned to kill insects. It could do the same for you.

9. Do not use large amounts of seeds, unless you know what you are doing and intend to give them away or sell them after they start to grow.

10. Do not get discouraged, if you forget to water them and they die or if you give them too much water and you drown them. Start over and build a regular habit taking care of them, and they will take care of you better than any pill, tablets, or medicine that your druggist or doctor can give you.

YOU ARE WHAT YOU EAT—

So let us eat young food, think young thoughts, do young things; in fact, let us live a little.

Remember — in all the seed sprouts, you will find the youth vitamin—Vitamin E.

HOW TO SPROUT

Now that you know all the rules — let's see how to sprout. We will tell you a good way, then we will tell you — go to the store and buy one of our sprouting trays.

A good method, with items you have around your home, is: (let us use Alfalfa seed, The King of Sprouts)

1. Take one tablespoonful of Alfalfa seeds and pour into a fruit jar with two cups of cool-warm water, about 70 degrees, let stand 12 hours. Be sure seeds go to the bottom and soak up the water.
2. Next day, tie a piece of Nylon over mouth of bottle, then pour the water out.
3. Every four hours during the day, fill the bottle with fresh water and then pour it out.
4. Be SURE you drain the water out of the bottle.
5. After three or four days of this, your bottle will be full of Alfalfa sprouts.
                         GOOD LUCK!!

PINTO BEANS

Every time I think of Pinto Beans I think of my Boy Scouting days when we were up at camp and we were served Chili and Beans. The next day the air was filled with gasses and comic remarks. That night out came the Chili and Beans again; also — out came the "Oh No's — Not beans again." Our Scout Leader held up his hand and said, "These beans are not the same, you try them." Sure enough, the next day no strange gasses. That night we asked him what was the difference. He only smiled and said, "We cooked them upside down." It was not until twenty years later that I found out what he had done. Now I am going to share his secret with you — he sprouted the beans for two days before he cooked them.

For a real Vitamin Treat, sprout your Chili Beans for 48 hours before cooking them, and everyone will say, "No gas, How come?" Then you can say, "I cooked them upside down — the gas went up — instead of down."

Sprouting of PINTO, NAVY, RED, CHILI and some others

Here is a real treat!

Sprout your Pinto Beans for 3 days, or until the bean sprout is one-half inch long, before cooking them in plain water. Do not add salt or any seasonings until the beans are cooked to the desired tenderness.

This secret is worth more than the price of this book and I will tell you why. Beans just do not cook fast in hard or mineral water. When you add salt or any flavorings to the water, you make the water hard and slow down the cooking time; so add all of the flavorings after you have cooked them.

You will notice that the odor of the sprouted pinto beans, when cooking, resembles the odor of fresh corn-on-the-cob. No kidding — try it — this is one reason why sprouted beans do not have the gas effect of just plain cooked beans. The gases have been washed out as you sprouted them.

For Best Results

Soak the beans you are going to use overnight and use one of our sprouting trays. However, you may want to just soak the beans and water them every 4 hours. This method has been used for years by those who make beans their main food diet.

We first learned of sprouting beans from a friend who traveled through Central America. The housewives were sprouting them, not really knowing the added nutritional value. They did know it made them taste better. They would only sprout them for two days; not long enough for the sprouts to really show but long enough to stop some of the stomach gas effects and swell the bean.

We now have perfected a better and cleaner method of sprouting. When you use our trays — you can wash the beans each time you water them and any dust, odor or dead beans can and will be washed away.

With the towel method, you let all this settle in the towel and if you are not careful, you might breed some healthy bacteria or mold. In real hot weather, soak a towel in water and place it over the beans to keep the beans moist — also to keep the dust and flies off; but rinse that towel every day in fresh water. I do this as I like to be clean with my food. If you place your tray on the drain board of your sink you will not forget to water them. Pour a quart or two of water over them every time you get a drink. If you use a towel over the tray, pour the water right on the towel. Be sure each day you BAPTIZE your beans four or five times.

We used the word "baptize" to impress you. To baptize means to immerse or place under the water. Do it.

Why?

You will be surprised at the delicious taste of the beans when sprouted. I like to take a small bowl full of the unseasoned beans and put some butter, salt and pepper on them. I eat these with delight and I still say they remind me of eating corn on the cob. Try it and see what you think.

Beans unsprouted never do compare with sprouted beans as to vitamins, minerals, live enzymes and life-saving amino acids. Besides, when you sprout the beans, you get more. Why? Because the beans swell up larger and a half-inch bean sprout has been added.

Beware, do not sprout your beans too long. You lose that fresh corn-like taste, and you may have a little trouble with the beans forming roots and leaves. The leaves and roots change the taste of the bean sprouts. I do not like it but maybe you will. Try it — what can you lose?

Another advantage of our sprouting trays over the towel method is that the beans have the best water drainage possible. There is no chance of rotting the bottom beans.

For bean treats — follow the recipes in our cook book.

For a real treat with any of our bean recipes, mix the beans. Use some white, some red, some pinto with navy and sprout them all together and cook them all together — blend the flavor — it is great — try it, you'll like it!

AGAIN WE ASK:
"Do you want to save money?"

WELL — sprout your beans and get everything — including good health.

Next time you buy a 15 oz. can of Pinto Beans, count them and you will find about 320 beans in the can. These DRY weigh about 4 ounces or one-fourth of a pound. In other words, one pound of dry pinto beans, after soaking and cooking, will make four 15-ounce cans of beans.

I priced some canned pinto beans and found the price averaged 15 cents a can. Four cans would cost you 60 cents.

One pound of DRY BEANS costs around 10 cents.

If you sprouted them for three days, you would have around four pounds of beans and more vitamins and minerals than you have ever had before.

Best of all, they will not be "SYNTHETIC VITAMINS" that lose their value after being on the shelf a period of time.

MUNG BEANS
A 5000 Year Old Secret

Mung Beans are probably the oldest known bean used for sprouting. The Chinese first started using them about 3,000 years before Christ. They are used in more ways in eating than any other bean. So be sure and read all the recipes on the use of MUNG BEANS.

From a two-ounce cup of Mung Bean seeds, you will have a Number 10 can full of fresh Mung Bean sprouts.

You will note that this number 10 can has a plastic bucket inside. The can acts as a light shield. Mung Beans should be grown in the dark.

Follow the directions and every five days you, too, may have this large can full of fresh sprouts for salads or any of the good recipes in the book.

We have the Chinese and the Japanese to thank for the knowledge of sprouting and the many ways of eating them.

Many people have tried to grow Mung Bean Sprouts and have been unhappy with their results. Now you can sprout Mung Beans to match the professional skills of the orientals. Anyone can do it simply and effortlessly with one of our Mung Bean Sprouting Kits.

"Sprouting" is the smart thing to do these days to help the ecology. Not only will you save money, but you will greatly increase the nutritional value of your food. It takes very little space, a very short time, and it is fun to grow your own live food so deliciously free of pesticides and preservatives.

We dare you to try it.

LEARNING THE SECRET:

After experimenting with many different trays, bottles, pans and anything a sprout would grow in, we finally asked a Chinese grower. He would not give us much help nor did he tell us much more than we already knew. So we kept asking and piecing little bits of talk together. Now we are able to grow the best tasting Mung Bean Sprouts you have ever tasted, up to six inches long.

All this took about three months of research, testing, growing and asking. Now we can give you the secret which is only common sense and reasoning when you stop to think it out.

HERE IT IS:

First — Let us stop and reason; what builds the character of a man? Is it not hard work — overcoming opposition? Right you are. This we will apply to our Mung Beans. Now remember that and what we told you in the book before: "You do not grow all seeds the same way." To get the results you want, you must treat each type of seed a little differently.

Second — What helps a man to create and concentrate? To be left alone, of course. How can anyone build, plan, or invent with everyone bothering or stirring him up? Right, no one. So let us apply this to our Mung Beans. Some of the other seeds need stirring up to get the results you want, (so do some people), but not Mung Beans.

Third — What helps a man to keep fit and regular? Lots of water. Your Mung Beans need far more water than any of the other seeds and also better drainage.

Fourth — If a man wants a healthy outdoor look, he will stay out in the sun. Those who stay inside do not brown. O.K., we want our Mung Bean Sprouts soft, white, yet crisp—so we raise them in the DARK.

Now that you have some ideas, let us apply them all to the growing of Mung Bean Sprouts.

Follow directions — carefully — you are not dealing with just any old bean. These are Mung Beans. You want the best sprouts that can be had, so they must be treated differently. If you go wrong, start over or you will have a mess.

—REMEMBER—

1. Get good seed. Mung Beans sometimes get small worms in them. You will know this when you place them in water. If they float, throw them away.

2. Place the amount you want to grow in a pan of water. Let us start with only one cup of beans in a two-quart pan.

3. Let hot water run over the beans for about five minutes. Do not use water any hotter than your hand will stand, because you are to put your hand in the pan of water and slowly swish the beans around.

This hot water does several things to the beans. 1st — it cleans the beans and floats the bad ones...2nd — it leaches the beans...3rd — it starts swelling the beans so that the water can penetrate and build up a growing supply of water. Some beans need this leaching process; others do not. If you cannot let the water run over the beans, change water four or five times.

4. Now place the beans in a warm place and let stand, covered with water, for 18 to 24 hours. This is longer than any other bean. If the water begins to ferment or stink, then change it. The water should be around 55 to 70 degrees. We do not want to cook the beans, or start them growing yet. We only want to build up a storage supply of water in the beans and swell them to split the covering.

5. Now place the beans in a specially built tub for growing. This is part of the secret. This tub is more like a small barrel than a tray. It should be deep and light tight, with excellent drainage. If Mung Beans do not have good drainage, they will sour fast. If this happens — throw them away and start over.

6. Do not place more than one inch of seeds in the bottom of the growing tub. You are not going into the selling of Mung Bean Sprouts — or are you? It is a good business. Think, now, if you have one inch of bean seeds

and they expand about 25 times to grow sprouts, you will need a deep tub.

7.   Over the top of your beans, place a strip of burlap folded several times. This cuts out the light and also helps hold water between watering. It also will move up as the beans grow. If you do not keep the light out, the sprouts will turn brown and green.

8.   Another secret — on top of the burlap, place a rock or small brick, or you may want to make a small bag and put some small one-half inch stones in it. This bag of stones should not be more than ½ inch thick and cover the inside of the tub. It will also move up as the bean sprouts grow. This is the opposition the beans must overcome. The weight of the rocks force the bean sprouts to grow thick, crisp and solid as they push up.

9.   Be sure to water the beans every two or three hours. Do this by pouring the water on top of the rocks. Do not disturb the sprouts by looking under the burlap. Let them grow and absorb the water. In the commercial growing houses, they have automatic sprinklers because Mung Beans do need plenty of water. They expand about 25 times their original size in five to seven days.

Be sure the water drains out well or they will rot in the stagnant water.

10. Be sure the growing room is warm, never under 70 degrees.

11. By force-growing the bean sprouts, (giving them plenty of water), you make it so the plant does not have to grow long roots trying to find water; all the energy goes to producing the sprouts. The roots have a different taste. You may like it. I do not mind it, but I do like the fresh sprout taste better.

12.   The final step is after 5 to 7 days. You dump the Mung Beans into your sink full of water, (COLD WATER), and rinse well. This rinsing makes the green bean covers come to the top of the water and you can skim them off. Sure, you can eat them if you want to; I don't. I like my bean sprouts white, crisp, thick and sweet. If you leave them sprouting too long — they will start to grow leaves and roots. This changes the taste a little.

WELL, there you have it.

If you want to save money—sprout your Mung Beans.

Never let Mung Beans sprout like those in the picture. They lose their flavor and become bitter.

The pie plate is placed on top of the can to help keep the light out. The burlap is placed on top of the beans right after you have soaked them overnight.

As the beans grow, they push the burlap up and out of the can. Never let this happen. When the burlap gets to the top of the can, eat your Mung Beans—they are long enough then.

If you want to make money—sell your Sprouts.

You will get about ten to one on your money — sell them.

SPROUTING RULES FOR FLAT TRAYS

We have tried several methods of sprouting and find that each type of seed needs a little different care to get the desired results.

So we designed a tray that would do the best job for most seeds and cost the least.

It is made of wood with a strong plastic screen bottom. WHY? Metal, glass or plastic trays act as radiators and draw the heat from the sprouts and dispel it into the room. This retards the growth of the sprouts.

It is also a cleaner way. It lets the seeds drain much better. When you place a towel in the bottom of the tray, you catch all of the dirt from the seeds and you also run the chance of collecting odors. If you do not change the towel once or twice during sprouting process, you might cultivate fungi or bacteria. This is important if you want to eat the sprouts right from the trays.

Another advantage of the wood and screen tray is that it floats in the water. NOW — to water your seeds well and clean them right, fill your pan or kitchen sink with fresh clean water and place the tray in it. Lift the tray in and out of the water four or five times and you will see the change in the color of the water. This is especially true when sprouting beans, you will not want them any other way. Also, if the tray slips out of your hands, the seeds have a greater chance of staying in the tray.

If you want to use a towel, place it on top of the sprouts and each day rinse it out with fresh water.

To wash your tray, let it sit in the sink with a little bleach in the water or if you wish, wash the tray with your dish soap, then rinse clean.

DIRECTIONS:

These directions are for most seeds. For the complete information, read the directions in each section of the book under each type of seed that you are going to sprout.

1. Soak most seeds for 12 hours. Seeds should be untreated and fertile. For best results, the water should be fresh and clean. Never over 80 degrees or under 50.
2. Place the seeds in the tray and then place tray in the sink full of water so that the seeds will spread level

This is what a good home-made sprouting tray looks like. It has the advantage of being made of wood. It floats, it is easy to clean, inexpensive to make or buy, has excellent drainage, it will last a long time, and you can make it to fit your needs.

Use nylon window screen for the bottom and do not worry about the nails rusting. The iron is good for the plants, and this is in turn good for you (so I have been told).

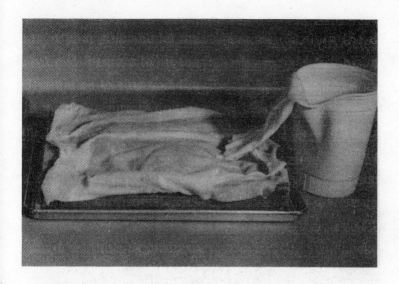

Never leave a tray of Sprouts on a flat surface —
the water will stagnate and rot the Sprouts.

Be sure there is an air space between the Sprouts
and whatever it is on.

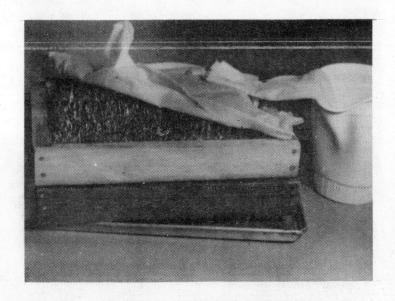

   If you are going to be gone all day and have no one
to water your sprouts, place a pot of water by your
tray. Then place a folded paper towel from tray to
water as shown. The water will slowly move through
the paper towel to the paper covering the sprouts as
needed and will keep the sprouts wet. We do this even
when we are home.
   You may even water 3 or 4 trays at once this way.
Or you may want to start a new crop every day. You
can this way — but be sure that you rinse them each
day to keep the sprout roots from going through the
screen and to keep them clean.

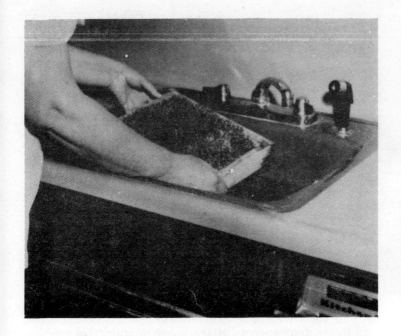

Each morning and night place the tray of sprouts in your sink full of cold water. Now rinse up and down so that the water goes through the sprouts, washing any dead seeds or seed pods away.

This will make sure the sprouts are clean, fresh, wet, and free of non-sprouting seeds that sometimes rot.

in the tray. Lift the tray out and let drain.

3. To water, place tray in a pan or your sink and let the
    seeds soak up the water they need. Be sure to lift the
    tray up and down four or five times to rinse off the
    dirt or any fungi that might form. Be sure to do this
    every 4 or 5 hours. Floating seeds are dry so sink
    them with your hand.

4. To drain tray, tilt on a slight angle until most of the
    water drains off. Seeds should be kept moist. Not
    soaking wet.

5. Place tray over a shallow pan or on the sink drain so
    that there is an air space under the tray. This lets
    the seeds drain and also helps to keep seeds warm
    by letting the air circulate around the tray.

6. Be sure — keep your sprouts warm, room tem-
    perature, and in a dark place.

7. For the green chlorophyll, place the tray of sprouts
    in the sunlight after the third day in the tray.
    Sprouts are ready at different times. Alfalfa 5 to 7
    days, Pinto Beans around 3 or 4.
    Be sure — clean the tray each time after use.

DEHYDRATED FOODS

There are many dehydrated foods on the store
shelves today. In fact, we have been using dried foods

for thousands of years and paid little attention to this. For example, all of your spices are some type of herb dried and powdered; most of your breakfast cereals, all of your storage grains and beans, your flour, cake mixes, and gelatin drinks or desserts; the list is almost endless.

It has only been since World War I that we have bottled or canned foods. Let us face it, dried foods have been used longer and are far safer for you to store and eat than wet pack.

WHY:

1—No metal can to rust or bottle to break.

2—They have not had all of the vitamins and minerals cooked out of them.

3—No sugar or sugar substitutes have been added.

4—No preservatives or poisons have been added to kill bacteria.

5—In commercial packing, sometimes weak solutions of Sulphide have been used to keep the color in the foods. This can be washed off by rinsing the dried foods just before adding water to reconstitute it to its original state.

Do not be alarmed at this, because you have been eating Sulphides ever since you started to buy those tasty French Fried Potatoes with your hamburgers.

If you ask a dealer how he keeps his potatoes so crisp and white, he either does not know or he says, "they dunk them in a solution of Potato Keep." Many producers use this for their fresh foods to keep the color for you. So be sure you rinse your fresh or dehydrated foods before eating them.

In case the food has been powdered or in too small of pieces to rinse, you may be sure that, as a rule, Sulphides were not used. Such foods are grain flour, potato flour, powdered milk, spices, powdered eggs, starch and corn meal.

DRYING FOODS:

There are three ways to dry or dehydrate foods:

1—Sun or Air Dried

This is used in most foreign countries today just the same as it was used hundreds of years ago and people are still buying products so dried. Such products as beans, tea, grains, and spices.

2—Heat Dried

This method is used where the product is to be stored for long periods of time and the water content is to be as low as possible.

3—Freeze Drying

This method is new and is a very good method because it quickly takes the moisture out and preserves the minerals, vitamins and color better than the other two methods—however, you cannot do this in your home without special equipment which costs a great deal.

If you live on a farm or have your own green house and raise your own food, you may want to dry some for storage. However, if you live in the city where it is impossible to grow your own, you still may save money and build up a storage supply of dried foods.

THIS IS HOW:

1—Be sure you buy from a reliable food supplier.

2—Be sure you rotate your food supply. For some reason, cans age and deteriorate after a period of time. It seems that this runs in three or four year cycles. In other words, a can could live 3, 6, 9, 12 or more years before dying. The food inside may be good indefinitely — but — because the can will let ozone and moisture in

— the food will spoil unless the can has been coated or protected against oxidization.

Bottling your dried food is not a complete answer because of cost, wasted space and breakage. Vacuum packing of dehydrated and freeze dried foods is the best method as air is removed from the can, then to keep the can from caving in, a nonpoisonous gas is put in the can and sealed. In this way not only are the weevil in the grain products destroyed by freezing, but their eggs as well. Should anything escape this, we do not think they could live without ozone in a vacuum packed can.

Rotate your food and use it—this way you can be sure it is safe and you will know how to use it when needed. One of the best reasons for using it is that you will save money when you buy in large cans. Dried foods keep very well in a covered container without refrigeration.

SPROUTS AND DRIED FOODS

All of our recipes can substitute dried foods if they have been reconstituted as directed on the can. You will find that by the addition of fresh sprouts, the food will be much tastier and delicious. The food value will be increased so much that we cannot put it into print. You will just have to try it to know for yourself.

Again—if you want to save money, really save money, use dehydrated foods and mix with freshly grown sprouts right from your own kitchen garden.

Why buy water — Buy food dried
Buy it in bulk
Use when needed and Sprout

The ideal self-preservation system is a green house with sprouting trays and drying racks. You then can live the year around from your own back yard.

SPROUTING METHODS

There are many sprouting methods on the store shelves—some made to sell and use, while others are made to sell with a fancy price because they look fancy. You choose which one you like best, they all will do something.

What we have tried to do on the next few pages is to show you that you do not have to buy a lot of fancy equipment to start sprouting.

South of the Border they have been using towels or blankets for years. In the Old Testament of the Bible they used pulse pots, or what we call sprouting pots. The ancient Americans, both South and North, never traveled without their seed pots. In Asia they used sacks; you may do the same as anyone of them.

I like the wood tray for most items such as alfalfa, pinto, soy, lentil, peas and grains of all types. I like the no. 10 can with the plastic bucket inside for mung beans, and glass bowls or trays for hot seeds like mustard and radish. You try them all and see which one you like best. The one you have the most success with—keep using. You will save money and gain health by eating fresh vitamins, minerals, life-saving enzymes and amino acids high in protein. So, let's start.

THE GLASS BOTTLE METHOD

This is the beginners method. You may in place of the plastic screen use a piece of nylon stocking or a fine woven window curtain. If you want to be fancy—get a piece of stainless steel screen and cut a round circle to fit into the lid of the bottle.

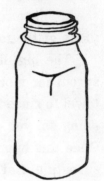

Now follow the directions for whatever you are going to sprout. See page 38.

The bottle method does have one big disadvantage; you do have to drain it extra carefully and water it more often. If you don't—you could have a swamp odor inside of the bottle. This will leave a disagreeable taste in your mouth and may turn you off of sprouting. Do not let this happen.

This method is best suited for alfalfa, wheat and small amounts of beans.

AFTER A FEW DAYS

DRAIN AND ALLOW TO STAND

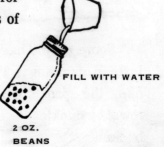

FILL WITH WATER

2 OZ. BEANS

THE TOWEL METHOD

This method works very well for red, pinto, soy, navy, small white and some of the other beans and seeds—even mung. I have seen people use burlap in place of the towel.

The big disadvantage is that most people cannot sprout for more than four days without picking up the towel to rinse the odor or the color out of the towel. In doing so, you break the tender sprouts, killing them. Once this happens, bacteria starts and you must stop sprouting. Eat them or give them to the chickens. Also there is a problem of keeping the sprouts wet without them souring because of lack of proper drainage.

Be sure that you wash the towel thoroughly each time before you start sprouting.

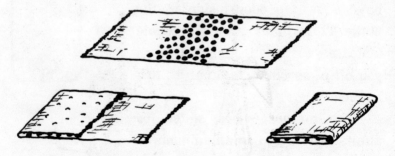

Some people have found it better to roll the towel instead of folding it. This is so they may tie the ends and hang the sprouts over a bucket of water and wet the towel by dunking it—letting the water drip back into the bucket.

THE SACK METHOD

This method works well with mung beans. If you use this method, be sure that the room is dark. Otherwise the roots will turn dark and the sprouts will turn brown and lose their flavor.

Some of the mung bean growers use this method. They have large cans; then after each dunking in water, they hang the sacks in the cans to drip with the lids put back on. This also keeps the moisture in the cans and helps to keep the sprouts wet.

The disadvantage is that with the sack out of sight, the sprouting is forgotten after about the second dunking, and one day an odor comes from someplace and then you remember —OH—BOY—MY—SPROUTS!! My Poor Mung Beans!

DIP
AND
LET
DRIP

AFTER A
FEW DAYS

THE FLOWER POT METHOD

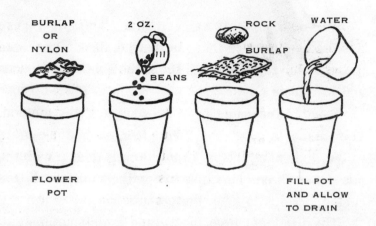

This is a very good method for sprouting mung beans. The clay pot holds the moisture and has good drainage, and at the same time allows room for the sprouts to expand up and out. Be sure you water often because the clay pot will absorb odors.

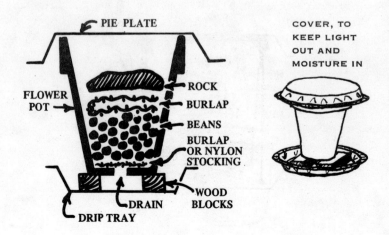

NO. 10 CAN METHOD

PIE PLATE
WATER‡
BURLAP

2 - 3 OZ.
BEANS

3 QT.
PLASTIC
BUCKET
WITH HOLES

NO. 10 CAN
[TO KEEP
LIGHT OUT]

PIE
PLATE

‡WATER, FILL BUCKET
AND ALLOW TO DRAIN,
THEN COVER WITH
PIE PLATE

This method I like best—and use. The can keeps the light out and does not look out of place on your kitchen sink. It also will last for a long time. It is easy to get and it costs nothing. Just buy a no. 10 can of some food item and cut the top and bottom out. Get a three-quart plastic bucket at any store for the inside. You can get these free when you buy a carton of ice cream or cottage cheese. See page 43 for instructions.

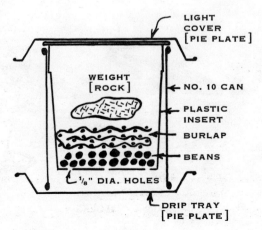

LIGHT
COVER
[PIE PLATE]

WEIGHT
[ROCK]

NO. 10 CAN

PLASTIC
INSERT

BURLAP

BEANS

1/8" DIA. HOLES

DRIP TRAY
[PIE PLATE]

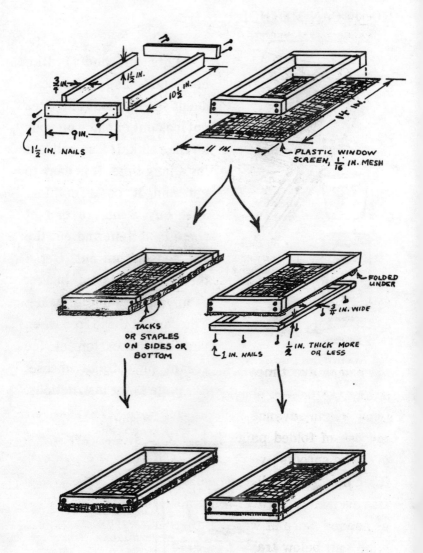

Make your own wood tray.

It is easy.

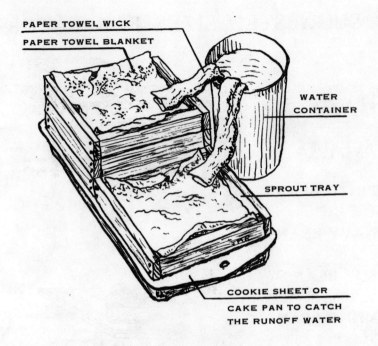

PAPER TOWEL WICK
PAPER TOWEL BLANKET
WATER CONTAINER
SPROUT TRAY
COOKIE SHEET OR CAKE PAN TO CATCH THE RUNOFF WATER

There are times when you cannot be with your sprouts when you should be at watering time. If you know this in advance, set up a self-watering station. By the use of folded paper towels and paper towels laid over the sprouts—you have your answer. We use it all the time. It is called "capillary action". The water travels from the water container to the sprouting trays as needed. Surplus water, if there is any, drops into the cake pan below trays.

It is so simple—I am surprised that I did not think of it before you did.

SUGGESTED SIZES FOR EATING

(Actual Sizes)

PLANT: **SEED:**   **SPROUT:**

ALFALFA

PINTO BEANS

NAVY BEANS

SOY BEANS

MUNG BEANS

GARBANZO
   BEANS

LENTILS

ALASKAN PEAS

WHEAT AND
TRITICALE
(ALSO OTHER
   GRAINS)

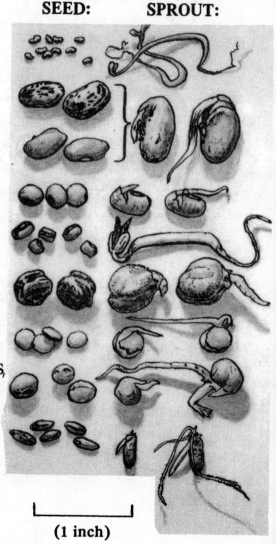

(1 inch)

Section II

COOKBOOK ON SPROUTS

A LIVE FOOD
Full of Vitamins and Minerals
Amino Acids and Live Enzymes

—with index—

Compiled by
Dorothy K. Reynolds

SEEING IS BELIEVING

And, you may believe this, because it IS a fact. All bean recipes can be improved by the use of sprouted beans. It just takes a little while longer to make what you want, but look what you get: better flavor, more vitamins, more minerals, more protein, more of everything including more bean plus a little bean sprout which more than doubles the amount of food.

YOU LIKE SAVING MONEY?
SPROUT YOUR BEANS

Sunflower seeds: shelled, salted, or roasted are delicious sprinkled over salad.

SPROUTS

Sprouts are always best when served fresh in a salad or eaten raw right from the growing trays.

All varieties of sprouts may be added to salads—whole or chopped.

Chopped or whole sprouts may be added to meat loaves, casseroles, soups, stews, and juices. Be sure that you add them just before serving to insure the crunchy goodness of the fresh sprout. Also, to prevent any loss of vitamins, minerals, amino acids or live enzymes.

Sprouts are delicious and healthful when steamed in a small amount of water in a covered pan for a short period of time. You may serve them with vinegar or some other mild seasoning.

Always drink your sprout juice within 10 minutes after making. This will prevent loss of vitamins.

SPROUTED WHEAT

We have said very little about sprouted wheat, yet it is one of the important life-saving sprouts.

There is a big difference in eating dry wheat or wheat products and sprouted wheat or slow-dried sprouted wheat and wheat grass.

The big difference is that dry wheat is chiefly made of carbohydrates, starch, proteins and if the wheat germ has not been removed, vitamin B's.

When you sprout wheat for three days, you add to the wheat: enzymes, amino acids, more vitamins, and minerals.

Now let the wheat grow 10 days and you add chlorophyll. You will lose some of the benefits of the fresh sprouts but you gain chlorophyll.

The two very best plants for chlorophyll are the wheat grasses and alfalfa. These two plants together make a green drink that cannot be equaled.

So, it depends upon what you want. Eat accordingly.

GREEN SALAD

1   head of lettuce, "broken"
2   cups of alfalfa sprouts
1   tomato cut in small pieces
1   onion cut in slivers

Top this with grated cheese, sharp or mild to your taste.

Always break lettuce to insure crispness.

ALFALFA GREEN SALAD

2   cups of alfalfa sprouts, "green"
½   cup of slivered onions
1   tomato, cut in small pieces
1   cucumber, cut in chips
2   stocks of celery, slivered
½   green pepper, slivered

You may vary the salad to your liking by adding lettuce, cabbage or cauliflower. You may want to make a conglomeration by adding everything.

Top this with your favorite dressing.

CHLOROPHYLL SPECIAL

10 outside leaves of lettuce, broken into small pieces.
2   cups of green alfalfa sprouts
½   cup green pepper, slivered
4   tops from celery sticks
6   green onions, chopped
4   outside leaves of cabbage, chopped
1   heaping tablespoonful of chopped parsley.

Top all this with your favorite dressing. Or for a change, steam for 5 minutes in a covered pan and serve it with vinegar or some other mild dressing. DO NOT COOK.

ALFALFA SPECIAL

2   cups alfalfa sprouts, chopped
1   diced avocado
1   diced cucumber
3   diced tomatoes

Toss and serve with or without your favorite dressing.

A SIMPLE SALAD

2 cups of alfalfa sprouts
1 tomato, slivered
1 onion, slivered, 2-inch size
    To this add any one or all of the following (or all?):
Not So Simple Salad
    Green peppers, green onions, cucumber chips,
lettuce, celery slivers, cabbage, cheese slivers,
cauliflower, apple diced, carrots diced, avocado diced,
raisins, etc.
    Toss and be sure to add your favorite dressing.

A RED SALAD

2 cups of alfalfa sprouts
1 cup of mung bean sprouts
1 cup of chopped red cabbage
1 diced tomato
1 large carrot, grated
1 cup of red onion slivers
¼ cup of diced red pepper
    Toss and serve with or without your favorite
dressing.

COLESLAW SPECIAL

½ head shredded cabbage
2 cups alfalfa sprouts
½ cup of chopped soybean sprouts
½ cup green pepper, slivered
1 2-inch onion, slivered
    Mix with a "tart" coleslaw dressing.

SPROUTED SOYBEAN SALAD

2 large apples, unpeeled and diced
2 large carrots, grated
½ cup of raisins, chopped or whole
1 cup of soybeans, sprouted and chopped
The soybeans give this salad a nut-like flavor. This salad is very high in Vitamin C, excellent in Vitamin A, B, G and E. It's full of Phosphorus and Iron. It is good!
Use your favorite dressing.

BEAN and CABBAGE SALAD

¼ teaspoonful caraway seed, sprouted
2 cups of finely chopped cabbage
2 cups sprouted beans, cooked, use your choice of: pinto, navy, kidney, etc.
1 tablespoon sugar
1 cup sour cream
½ cup of grated onions
1 teaspoonful vinegar
Chill cabbage and beans; mix and add onion, combine the sour cream, vinegar and sugar, then pour over salad, toss and top with caraway seeds. Makes 4 to 6 servings.

POTATO SALAD SUPREME

To double the vitamin and food value of your favorite potato salad, add (1 cup) of chopped sprouted soybeans.

For "Health Sakes," use sprouted seeds as much as possible.

SWEET and SOUR SALAD

2   cups boiled, sprouted navy beans (cooled)
¼   cup of cider vinegar
½   cup of salad oil
½   onion chopped finely
½   teaspoon of dry mustard
1   teaspoon of salt
2   tablespoons of sugar
4   sprigs of parsley
½   onion in rings or slivered
¼   green pepper, slivered

Heat vinegar, dry mustard, salt and sugar for one minute. Cool and add salad oil. Then mix beans thoroughly in this marinade. Toss with chopped onion and garnish with onion rings, green pepper, and the parsley. Makes 3 to 4 servings.

POTATO SPROUT PATTIES

4   cups mashed potatoes
¼   square of butter
1   egg, salt and pepper
½   cup of either mung beans, soybeans, or lentils finely chopped. Mix this and form into patties and dip into flour, then beaten egg and fry in hot oil until very brown. Drain well and serve.

SPROUTED LENTIL SALAD

½ pound sprouted lentils
2½ cups of water
1 onion studded with 2 whole cloves and 1 bay leaf
    Bring this to boil, and simmer about 30 minutes, when tender drain excess water and save for use in soup. Remove onion and bay leaf and place lentils in a large bowl that has been rubbed with a piece of garlic. When cool add:
1 cup of alfalfa sprouts
1 cup of mung bean sprouts
½ cup of slivered celery
¾ cup chopped onion (red)
    Serve with your favorite dressing livened up with chopped chives and 1 teaspoon of dill seed. Serves six.

MUNG BEAN SALAD

    Here is a salad that I could make a whole meal of. It is one of my favorites. Be sure you try it. Sometimes we leave the soybeans out, but the added vitamins it gives should not be overlooked.
2 cups sprouted mung beans
2 cups alfalfa sprouts
1 large onion, diced
1 tomato, slivered
½ cup of chopped soybeans sprouted 3 days
    Top this with your favorite dressing.
    Now if you are sprouting your own seeds, this vitamin, mineral, healthful salad will cost you only about 15 cents for a family of 5. Not only that, but this salad is a live food with no poison sprays, fresh from your garden.
    Beats eating a dead head of lettuce; tastes better too.

CURRIED SUCCOTASH SALAD

2   cups cooked whole kernel corn
2   cups sprouted beans, cooked
½   cup chopped onion, medium
½   cup celery, chopped
¼   cup green pepper, chopped
¼   diced pimento
½   cup raw sugar or honey
1   tablespoon of curry powder
1   stick of cinnamon (broken)
1   teaspoon of whole cloves
1   teaspoon of celery seeds
1   teaspoon of salt
1   cup of cider vinegar

Drain liquids from cooked corn and beans and save.

Combine corn and beans, onions, celery, green pepper, and pimento in a bowl.

Combine ½ cup of liquid with the sugar or honey, curry powder, cinnamon, cloves, salt, celery seeds and vinegar in a medium saucepan. Heat, stirring constantly to boiling; simmer 10 minutes, strain over vegetable mixture; cool, chill and serve.

Use your favorite sprouted bean.

COOKED SOYBEAN SPROUTS

1 pound of soybeans sprouted and cooked in small amount of water 3 to 10 minutes.

2 tablespoons of butter in a heavy pan, melt and add the sprouts and season with one teaspoon powdered vegetable broth; add small amount of soy sauce, stir until well blended and serve at once.

SCRAMBLED EGGS and SPROUTS

2 eggs
¼ cup of chopped onions
¼ cup of chopped alfalfa or mung bean sprouts
1 heaping tablespoon of grated cheese

Scramble eggs with onions and when almost set, add chopped sprouts and grated cheese. Serve immediately.

Substitute chopped, sprouted soybeans in place of the alfalfa.

SUKIYAKI

¾ lb. round or sirloin steak cut in pieces about 1 inch wide and 2 inches long.
1 bunch of green onions, cut in 1-inch pieces, use the tops also.
2 dry onions, sliced
6 sticks of celery, sliced diagonally
2 large carrots, sliced diagonally
2 cups mung bean sprouts, (whole)
¾ cup of soy sauce
¾ cup of brown sugar
1 cup water

Heat skillet to high temperature, add 2 tablespoons of oil; add meat and stir a few seconds. Add soy sauce, sugar, water and bring to a boil. Add carrots and dry onions and cook covered for 3 minutes more. Add celery then cover and cook 3 more minutes. Add green onions and mung bean sprouts. Let stand a few seconds. Serve immediately over rice. Serves 10.

SPANISH COOKING

Enchiladas:
Next time you make them, try replacing the lettuce with alfalfa or mung bean sprouts. What a Treat!
Burritos:
Next time you make them, try fresh sprouts topped with cheese.
Tacos:
One of my favorite tacos is: fill the tortilla with mung beans and alfalfa sprouts topping this with grated cheese and a little hot sauce. Try it.

Our tacos are always good filled with Dorothy's Sprouted Pinto Beans, Chili topped with alfalfa sprouts, grated cheese and a little hot sauce. See our Chili Recipe.

TACO SANDWICHES

Take bread dough and roll into a large round tortilla. Fry in hot oil until lightly browned on each side. Drain and fold in half.

Fill as you would a taco: meat or chili beans, alfalfa sprouts, tomatoes, and cheese. Use sprouted beans.

TAMALE PIE

Here is a recipe you will find no other place than in this book. It is good!

2 cups sprouted corn
3 cups of juiced tomatoes
2 large red chili peppers, diced
1 cup corn meal, uncooked
4 buds of garlic, cut up fine
1 large onion, diced
2 cups ripe olives, diced
2 pounds pork sausage
2 cups of milk
4 eggs, beaten
¾ teaspoon of salt

Fry sausage, drain, add garlic; to this, add tomato juice and red peppers plus 1 cup water, boil. Then add everything else and cook in a slow oven one to one and one-half hours. Serves 10.

JUST OLD CHILI

10 cups sprouted pinto beans, kidney or chili beans
2 pounds of ground beef
1 cup cooking oil
4 Mexican peppers, diced
2 quarts of water
2 tablespoons salt
2 tablespoons sugar
2 cups of diced onions
1 quart of cooked tomatoes
1 tablespoon of chili powder

Fry the meat in the oil until brown. Then add everything to it. Cook for about two hours.

This is basic chili. We have improved it by the use of sprouted beans.

SPROUTED BEAN CHILI

This is Dorothy's special Chili recipe. The basic part came from one of her friends in Mexico. She improved it by the use of sprouted beans, and carob.

Carob is used in place of chocolate. If you cannot find carob, use 1 ounce of chocolate. You will find carob in most health food stores.

2   large onions, chopped fine
1   bud garlic, chopped fine

NOW brown these in 2 tablespoons of shortening. Then add:

1   pound of ground beef and brown it also.
    Now add:
2   tablespoons chili powder
½   tablespoon of flour
1   teaspoon of cumin
1   teaspoon of marjoram
2   tablespoons sugar
½   tablespoon salt
1   No. 2 can of tomatoes
2   cups of water
1   quart of sprouted pinto beans or chili beans, cooked
1   ounce of carob, grated
    Simmer for about 2 hours.

For sauce leave meat out and make meat balls separately in a baking dish.

Simmer this sauce until thick, then pour over meat and bake a half hour at 350 degrees.

Serve this with corn meal cakes or crackers sprinkled with butter, paprika and salt.

WHEAT SPROUT CHILI

In a large heavy-duty skillet put 2 tablespoons of salad oil and brown 1 pound of ground beef. To this add:

¾ cup chopped onion
2 garlic cloves, minced
2 cups ground, dry, uncooked wheat sprouts
6 teaspoons of chili powder
1 teaspoon of salt
¼ teaspoon of pepper
½ teaspoon of oregano
¼ teaspoon of cayenne pepper
¼ teaspoon of marjoram
¼ teaspoon of cumin
5 cups bouillon
1 cup tomato puree

Cover and simmer over low heat for about 1 hour stirring often to enhance the flavor. Let stand awhile to blend the flavors. You can reheat in an oven at low temperature if you ever have any left over.

WHEAT SPROUT HASH

2   large onions, diced
2   green peppers, diced fine
3   tablespoons shortening
1   pound hamburger
2   cups canned tomatoes
1   cup cooked sprouted wheat
1   teaspoon chili powder
1   teaspoon salt
¼   teaspoon pepper

Cook onion and green pepper in shortening until onions are yellow, add hamburger and cook. Add tomatoes, wheat, and seasoning and place in a casserole, cover and bake for 45 minutes at 375 degrees. Serves 5.

Sprout your wheat for 5 days and you will get 10 times more value from them.

RAISIN BARBECUE WHEAT

2   cups boiling water
½   teaspoon salt
1   cup cracked sprouted wheat, dried

Cook over low heat, about 30 minutes.

Heat ½ cup of raisins in 1 teaspoon of chili powder and 2 tablespoons of butter until glazed; toss in with the hot cooked wheat. Add ½ teaspoon of salt, 2 tablespoons chopped green onions and 2 tablespoons of chopped pimento. Serves 4. Delicious with Chicken or Spare Ribs.

CREAMED VEGETABLE MONTEREY

2   cups sprouted peas, cooked
2   cups corn sprouted cooked
½   teaspoon salt, pepper, if desired
1   package of dry onion soup mix
    Combine the peas, corn, soup mix, salt and pepper in a medium size saucepan, heat to boiling and drain. If you like, you can serve it with a cheese sauce. Serves 6.

WHEAT MEAT STEW

1   pound of stew meat, diced (if you like, meat balls).
Brown in 2 tablespoons of oil. ADD:
1¼ quarts of water and simmer stew meat 2½ hours.
Hamburger meat balls ½ hour. ADD:
1   cup cracked sprouted wheat uncooked
½   teaspoon salt
1   bay leaf
    Add water if needed. Cook for 20 minutes more; add the following vegetables that have been cooked in another pan:
¼   cup of onions, diced
2   cups diced potatoes
2   cups diced carrots
    Serves 6. Serve it hot.
    If desired you can thicken with flour. You may replace the meat with fish or poultry.

WHEAT SPROUTS WITH CHEESE

2   cups boiling water
½   teaspoon of salt
1   cup cracked sprouted wheat, dried
    Cook over low heat about 30 minutes. ADD:
1   cup grated cheese
2   small cans of tomato puree.
    Add more water if necessary and heat in 350 degree oven until cheese melts. Serves 5.

VEGETABLE and WHEAT

    Use the same recipe for Wheat Sprouts with Cheese, but omit the cheese and add the following when you add puree:
¼   green pepper, slivered
¼   cup of chopped onion
¼   cup of chopped parsley
½   teaspoon of sugar, salt to taste

WHEAT MEAT LOAF

1   pound hamburger
½   pound pork sausage
1   medium onion
½   teaspoon salt
¼   teaspoon pepper
2   eggs
2½ cups cooked, sprouted wheat, cracked
1   cup tomato juice or milk
    Mix and place in greased loaf pan and bake 1 hour at 400 degrees. Serves 8.
    Serve plain or with tomato sauce.

SALMON WHEAT LOAF

2½ cups cooked, sprouted wheat
1 can salmon, drained
2 eggs
½ cup liquid, use the salmon juice and add milk
2 tablespoons sweet pickles, chopped
¼ cup chopped onion
2 tablespoons vinegar
½ teaspoon salt
¼ teaspoon pepper

Mix and place in greased loaf pan and bake at 350 degrees for 1 hour. Serves 6 to 8.

Serve with lemon or tartar sauce.

DANISH WHEAT MEAT BALLS

2 pounds ground beef
2 small onions, chopped fine
¼ teaspoon garlic powder
2 eggs, salt and pepper to taste
2 cups finely cracked sprouted wheat, cook dry
4 tablespoons canned milk

Mix well and form into patties or balls. Fry in a small amount of shortening until brown on all sides. Simmer 10 minutes in a small amount of brown sauce.

BROWN SAUCE

2   tablespoons flour
2   tablespoons margarine
Stir and cook until browned. Remove from heat about a minute. Then slowly pour in two cups of cold water. Place over heat and stir until smooth.

To convert this to Spanish style cooking, omit the brown sauce and cook patties or meat balls in 1 can of tomato sauce and 4 tablespoons hot water.

Season this sauce if you desire.

SPROUTED WHEAT PANCAKES

1   cup cracked, sprouted wheat
1½ cups water. Soak wheat overnight; then ADD:
2   cups flour
2   teaspoons salt
1   tablespoon baking powder
2   tablespoons sugar
¼   cup cooking oil
1½ cups whole milk
Stir until batter is smooth. Cook on hot, greased griddle.

Serve hot with butter and syrup. Serves 5.

WHEAT CAKES

1 cup whole wheat flour
¼ cup coarse-ground, sprouted (slow-dried) whole wheat
3 teaspoons baking powder
3 tablespoons sugar
¾ teaspoon salt
3 tablespoons drippings or oil
½ cup sprouted, dried chopped soybeans
3 eggs, well beaten
1¼ cups milk (or more)

Stir together dry ingredients. Combine eggs and milk, then stir into dry ingredients along with drippings. Mix only until blended.

For lighter pancakes, separate eggs. Beat yolks until fluffy; add to batter. Fold in stiffly beaten egg whites just before cooking.

Bake on lightly greased griddle until golden brown.
This batter makes good waffles also.
Makes 12 four-inch pancakes.

Cooked wheat sprouts can be used to replace bread crumbs, crackers, or cereals, when making stuffings in poultry, or in meat and fish loaves.

You may want to slow dry them and coarse grind first.

Wheat sprouted until the sprout is as long as the kernel itself can be dried and ground and used in the following recipe:

2 cups boiling water
½ teaspoon salt
1 cup cracked, sprouted wheat

Add wheat to boiling salt water. Cook over low heat for about 30 minutes. Remove from heat and let stand covered for 10 minutes. Serves 5.

There is nothing better than this for a breakfast cereal. You may want to use it whole kernel. You then can use them right from the tray.

Next time you think you want mashed potaotes, use the recipe above. You will be surprised how good it is with gravy or butter on it.

WHEAT-RAISIN PUDDING

Combine in a baking dish:
2½ cups cooked, sprouted wheat that has been dried and cracked
3 cups rich milk
1½ cups water
1½ cups evaporated milk
½ teaspoon salt
½ cup seedless raisins
½ cup honey or brown sugar
¼ teaspoon mace

Cover and bake in oven at 325 degrees for 45 minutes; remove cover and continue baking uncovered for another 45 minutes or until nicely browned. Stir once or twice.

Serves 6.

SOUPS

Make your favorite soups and replace the rice and the barley with cracked, slow-dried, sprouted wheat.

DATE-WHEAT BREAD

1 cup dates
1 cup boiling water
1 teaspoon baking soda
1 cup raw sugar
1 tablespoon butter
½ cup cracked, slow-dried, sprouted wheat
2 cups whole wheat flour
1 teaspoon baking powder
¼ teaspoon salt
½ cup chopped, sprouted and dried soybeans

Cut dates in small pieces and cover with boiling water, soda and let it cool. Then add all other ingredients, mix and place in a greased and lightly floured loaf pan. Bake 1 hour at 375 degrees.

You do not have a sprouter?

We have them. Starter Kit only $5.00.

SPROUTED WHOLE WHEAT BREAD

3   packages of dry yeast, dissolved in 1 cup of warm water.
    Then add:
4   cups warm water
1   tablespoon salt
¾   cup molasses or honey
5   tablespoons vegetable oil
1½ cups dry powdered milk
6   cups whole wheat flour
    Beat all this until well mixed, then add:
2   cups sprouted whole wheat, whole or dried and ground. As you knead, add enough flour to make a soft, elastic dough, then place dough in a large pan and brush top with oil, then cover with a clean dish cloth and let it rise in a warm place until it doubles its size. Then:

Push down and let rise again. Then:

Divide dough into 4 or 5 parts (according to pan size). Mold into loaves and place in greased bread pans. Place pans in a warm place and cover with a towel until it doubles in bulk.

Place in a pre-heated oven and bake for 15 minutes at 400 degrees. Then lower the heat to 350 degrees and bake another 45 minutes.

Cooled loaves may be frozen and kept in deep freeze.

APPLESAUCE NUT BREAD

1   large orange
½ cup seedless raisins
⅛   cup canned or fresh applesauce
¾ cup finely-cracked, slow-dried wheat sprouts
1¾ cups whole wheat flour
2   teaspoons baking powder
1   teaspoon baking soda
1   cup raw sugar
½ teaspoon salt
½ cup chopped, sprouted and dried soybeans
1   egg
2   tablespoons melted butter
    Squeeze juice from orange and grind pulp and rind.

Then add all other ingredients and place in a greased loaf pan which has been lined with wax paper. Bake at 325 degrees for 1 hour or until loaf is nicely browned and begins to shrink from the pan.

WHOLE WHEAT CAKE

Make a brown liquid by browning 1 cup of sugar in a pan. Then pour 1 cup of water over it and simmer until dissolved. Cool and save.

¼ cup sprouted, dried, ground whole wheat flour
1¾ cups regular whole wheat flour
2   tablespoons powdered milk
2   eggs
2   teaspoons baking powder
1   teaspoon vanilla
½   teaspoon salt
½   cup shortening
¾   cup honey or 1 cup sugar
½   cup of the reserved brown liquid plus 1 cup of water
   Blend dry ingredients, cream shortening. Add honey, eggs, and vanilla. Blend together with dry ingredients and water. Bake at 350 degrees. Cook for 30 minutes. Next, make the frosting.

FROSTING

¾ cup of butter
1 cup sugar
½ cup brown liquid left from cake
   Boil until hard ball stage; whip until thick then add ½ cup of sprouted dried soybeans chopped like nuts.

JUICES

Liquify finely chopped alfalfa in fruit or vegetable juice.
   Small amounts of any sprouts may be used in this manner.

QUICK ALFALFA PICKUP

In blender, liquify 1 cup of alfalfa sprouts with 2 cups pineapple or orange juice. Sweeten to taste. You can add 2 tablespoons of chopped, sprouted soybeans or almonds, or you may use any nut butter.

You can replace the nuts in any recipe with chopped, sprouted soybeans. This will also add Vitamin C, etc.

Chopped or whole sprouts may be added to meat loaves, casseroles, soups, stews, and all types of salads. Always add them just before serving to insure crunchy goodness and to prevent vitamin loss.

A new and delightful taste treat is chopped sprouted soybeans added to peanut butter for making sandwiches.

Chopped, sprouted soybeans added to pancakes are extra good.

Try them in cookies, cake recipes and also add them to your breakfast cereals. Your children will think they are nuts.

Add the sprouts of mung, lentil or soybean to your favorite bean recipe. You may also add them to your split pea recipes and to all pasta dishes.

Try sprouts sauteed with onions or peppers. Also try with tomatoes.

EGG FOO YUNG

Here's a great recipe we know you will like. It was given to us by Mrs. L. H. Magar.

4 or 5 eggs, beaten
1   medium onion, minced
1   green pepper, minced
1   tablespoon soy sauce
¼   teaspoon salt
½ or 1 lb. bean sprouts
½ cup celery, minced

Combine eggs, onions, green peppers, soy sauce and salt. Chop bean sprouts slightly, add and mix well. Cover bottom of frying pan with salad oil to a depth of 1 inch. Heat, drop egg mixture into oil by spoonfuls until golden brown, turning once. Drain on absorbent paper.

Then pour off all but 3 tablespoons of oil. Make a sauce by blending 3 tablespoons flour with oil and add 2 cups of water. Cook until thick, stirring constantly. Add soy sauce to taste. Serve over patties.

A good accompaniment is rice, chicken soup and pineapple chunks.

CHINESE COOKED BEAN SPROUTS

Chop one medium-size onion and cook in frying pan in ½ cup of butter or a little water until soft. Add a little diagonally cut celery in ½ inch slices. When soft add 3 or 4 cups of cleaned, drained, bean sprouts, green pea sprouts, wheat sprouts or rye sprouts.

Add a can of undiluted mushroom soup mixed with a can of chicken broth; you may want to thicken this with arrowroot flour.

For a tasty meal add 1 or 2 cans of (5 oz.) sliced chicken pieces and slivered almonds, serve on mound of hot rice or crisp chinese noodles.

Add soy sauce or serve it with a bottle of soy sauce at the table.

For this recipe we may thank Mrs. Virginia N. Straup. We tried it and it is great.

CHOW-MEIN

2 cups soybean sprouts
2 cups onions, sliced
4 tablespoons margarine or if you prefer, oil
2 cups of cooked meat; beef, veal, lamb, or pork
1 can mushrooms with liquid
   Season to taste and thicken with flour.

Cook sprouts 10 minutes. Fry sprouts in fat or oil until brown, add cooked sprouts, diced meat and chopped mushrooms with liquid. Add water from sprouts and more water if necessary to cover. Season as desired and add soy sauce. Thicken mixture with a small amount of flour (whole wheat preferred), cover and cook 10 minutes.

Serve with noodles or rice.

SWEET and SOUR SPARERIBS or PORK CHOPS

2 pounds of meat
2 tablespoons brown sugar
2 tablespoons corn starch
½ teaspoon salt
¼ cup vinegar
1 cup pineapple juice
¼ cup of water
1 tablespoon soy sauce
1 clove garlic, mashed
¼ teaspoon ground ginger
1 cup undiluted consomme (can use broth or bouillon)
¼ cup onion, diced
1 8 oz. can pineapple chunks
3 carrots, cut diagonally
2 stalks celery, cut diagonally
8 oz. mung bean sprouts

Cover meat with boiling salted water, cover and simmer 1 hour. Drain, brown in fat. Mix all ingredients except the vegetables. Cook till "crispy tender", then add mung bean sprouts and serve immediately over fluffy rice.

SPROUTED LENTIL BAKE

1   pound of sprouted lentils
1   large onion, diced
¼   teaspoon cloves
½   teaspoon marjoram or thyme
5   cups water
2   teaspoons salt

Heat to boiling on top of stove, let simmer 30 minutes. Then add:

½   cup chili sauce or catsup
¼   cup molasses
2   tablespoons brown sugar
1   teaspoon dry mustard
¼   teaspoon worcestershire sauce

Sprinkle top with bacon flavored soy bits. You may use weiners or diced bacon.

Cover and bake for 1 hour at 350 degrees. Uncover and brown.

This makes complete meal with whole wheat bread and a tossed sprout salad. Makes 6 one-cup servings.

LENTILS OLE'

1   pound of lentils, sprouted
5   cups water
3   teaspoons salt

Gently simmer about 30 minutes in a covered heavy pot and when tender, remove from heat and do not drain.

Place 2 tablespoons oil in a large pan.

1   large onion, diced
1   clove garlic, minced

Add this to hot oil and cook until onion is clear, then add 1 pound of ground round, or sausage. Brown and stir to break up. Pour off excess fat and add to the lentils.

Then add:

2   cans tomato sauce
2   cooked yams or sweet potato, diced
1   can of pears, diced or fresh, if you prefer
1   can of pineapple chunks

Cover and simmer until the pears are tender: about 15 minutes.

Minus the meat, this will make a very good side dish to serve with Pork or Ham.

A delicious meal in one dish — serves 6 to 8.

SPROUTED LENTIL CURRY

1   pound sprouted lentils
5   cups water
2   teaspoons salt

Add curry powder to taste then, bring to boil and simmer about 30 minutes. Drain and keep warm.

Serves 6 to 8.

CHICKEN CURRY

Use the Lentil Curry recipe and add the following:
1 large onion, diced or slivered
4 tablespoons margarine
   Simmer until onions are tender, then add:
1 large can of Cream of Chicken soup undiluted
   Add to this some extra cooked chicken. To serve:
   Arrange lentils in a circle around the edge of a serving platter, pour curry in the center.
   To make TUNA CURRY, use the recipe above, only leave out the chicken and add cooked tuna fish.
   You may want a small side dish to serve with your curry of chopped peanuts, cashews, green onions, crisp-crumbled bacon, chopped hard boiled egg or watermelon and pickles.

LENTIL BURGERS

Cook lentils as in the Sprouted Lentil Curry recipe.
   Then add:
2 cans of tomato soup
1 pound of hamburger
½ teaspoon barbecue sauce
½ teaspoon oregano
1 onion, diced
1 button garlic
   Cook until meat is done. Serve in burger buns or over rice or as you wish.

SOYBEAN-BACON BITS

Sprout some soybeans. Chop and fry in bacon fat, then when brown, drain on a paper towel.

You can use these bits to flavor salads, eggs, and any place you would use bacon.

LENTIL SALAD

Lentil salad can be a hearty meal in itself. You can add as you go along; cheese wedges, slices of tomato, chopped or whole nuts, onion rings, smoked meat and so forth.

Lentils go well with anything; fruits, vegetables, or meats. You may eat them raw or cooked with a little butter.

PEANUT BUTTER SANDWICH

Spread your sandwich then sprinkle with chopped soybeans and add a thick layer of alfalfa sprouts. For a real treat, mix some diced onions with the alfalfa sprouts.

"GREEN" RICE

Cook rice in double amount of chicken broth. Boil gently about ½ hour until dry and fluffy. Then add:
Soybean sprouts or mung bean, chopped or whole
chopped green onions
chopped green peppers
chopped parsley or flakes
Mix well and serve.

MAIN DISH—SOYBEAN-RICE CASSEROLE

Boil sprouted soybeans until tender. Boil unpolished rice in a different pan. (Use twice as much water as rice). Boil slowly about 25 or 30 minutes. Mix equal parts of both, then add tomato sauce and cubes of nut meat or meat (hamburger or left-over roast). Mix together and place in oven. Bake for 45 minutes slowly, 350 degrees. Uncover to brown the last 10 minutes.

TRIPLE SPROUT STEW

2 pounds stew meat, browned, cover with water, simmer until tender. Then cut celery, onions, potaotes, and carrots into large chunks and simmer until tender crisp.

Thicken if desired, and just before serving add:
8   oz. of mung beans sprouted
8   oz. of lentil beans sprouted
8   oz. of soybeans sprouted

Sprinkle with parsley and serve. You can substitute hamburger for the stew meat.

CANDIED BEANS with NUTS and APPLES

4   cups sprouted navy beans, cooked and drained
2   canned pimentos
2   medium sized apples
2   tablespoons chopped nutmeat
1   tablespoon brown sugar
1   tablespoon butter or bacon drippings
      Cook beans and drain.
      Chop the pimento, core and dice the unpeeled apples. Mix beans with pimento and apples then season and put into well-greased baking pan or dish.
      Sprinkle with sugar and nutmeats and dot with fat; now bake uncovered in hot oven for 10 minutes.

CONFECTION

   Grind together:
1   cup sprouted wheat
1   cup almonds or cashews
1   cup seeded raisins
      Salt to taste, one pinch
      Mix well and roll into small balls. Roll these in coconut.

No food storage program is complete without a sprouter kit. In time of emergency — to conserve on water — use the same water over and over. However, we recommend using fresh water each time.

TO COOK WHOLE TRITICALE:

OVERNIGHT METHOD

Pour 1 cup Triticale into 3 cups boiling water with 1 teaspoon of salt. Boil for 10 minutes. Turn off heat and let stand overnight with lid on. In the morning cook for about 15 minutes. Serve it with sugar and milk or try it with fruit and honey.

Cooked Triticale can be used in place of potatoes and served with gravy or butter.

Triticale can be cooked in the morning by letting it cook slowly for one-half hour to 1 hour, instead of the overnight method.

Cracked Triticale will cook in 20 to 30 minutes.

Sprouted Triticale maybe cooked or eaten without cooking. Triticale maybe ground into flour and used in breads or pastries.

Cracked Triticale or rolled Triticale is an excellent extender for meat and casseroles.

Triticale may be used in any of the wheat recipes — use it as you would wheat.

IMPROVED GRANOLA

Use it as a Breakfast Food or for a between-meal snack.

4 cups of rolled grain (your choice of Oats, Barley, Wheat or Rye)
1 cup of unsweetened cocoanut
1 cup of natural wheat germ
¼ cup of cooking oil (preferably Peanut Oil)
¾ cup of honey
1 teaspoon of vanilla

To increase the protein and mineral content, sprout 1 cup of soy beans only three days, dry and grind into bits.

Thoroughly mix together, spread on a cookie sheet, bake at 300 degrees for 20 minutes stirring occasionally while baking.

After cooling, add any or all of the following:
¼ cup sunflower seeds
¼ cup almond or pecans coarse chopped
¼ cup sesame seeds

If you find this mixture too course for your teeth, place in a blender and reduce to a granular mixture. Then add:
½ cup raisins or any other dried fruits such as Banana, currants, apples, etc.

For breakfast serve with milk—for between-meal snacks, eat a small dish full.

Store in a tightly lidded container and keep refrigerated, because you have not added any poison to kill bacteria.

HARDY SPROUTED LENTIL SOUP

1½ cups sprouted lentils
1   Onion chopped
¼   cup cubed salt pork
1   cup chopped celery
½   cup diced carrots
1   bay leaf
1   beef bouillon cube
2   cups water
1 to 2 tbsp. vinegar

Put onion and pork in a sauce pan and saute onion until translucent—add lentils and 3 cups of water—Mix—then add all the other ingredients except the vinegar. Cover and simmer 2 to 3 hours or until lentils are tender.

Before serving remember to remove Bay leaf and adjust seasonings. Add vinegar. You may serve it with sprouted mung beans and chopped little green onions and chopped parsley sprinkled on top.

WHEAT AND LENTIL MEAT LOAF

1¼ cup of wheat sprouted—dried and cracked
1   egg
1½ tsp. salt
⅛ tsp. pepper
¾ tsp. sage
2   tbsp. Worcestershire sauce
¼ cup chopped onions
¼ cup ketchup
1   lb. ground beef
1   cup sprouted lentils
½ cup milk

Blend ingredients together and turn into loaf pan or shape into loaf in a shallow baking dish. If desired spread surface with thin layer of ketchup. Bake at 350 degrees for about 1 hour or until nicely browned—makes 8 servings.

WHEAT SPROUTED PILAF

2   cups cooked wheat sprouts
3   tbsp. shortening (oil or margarine)
¼ cup chopped onion
1   tsp. salt
3   cups bouillon or soup stock

Cover the wheat sprouts with water and cook until wheat is soft to your liking.

Melt shortening in a large frying pan—saute wheat and chopped onions about 5 minutes. Add salt and simmer until liquid is absorbed—about 20 minutes.

If a less cruncy pilaf is desired—use cracked wheat instead of whole wheat. Makes 6 to 8 servings.

This is a good replacement for potatoes. If you add meat or fish and top it with cheese, it may be used as a main dish. Serve it with a Sprout Salad.

RICE AND SPROUT MEDELEY PILAF

½   cup chopped celery
1   chopped large onion
1   large or 2 medium carrots chopped
     Saute in 4 tbsp.butter or margarine until soft. Stir in
1 cup of sprouted wheat or triticale or any other grain
that has been sprouted only 2 days. Continue to stir until
slightly brown. Add 2½ cups of chicken broth. Cover
and simmer 45 minutes or until sprouted grains are
cooked to your liking and liquid is absorbed. Remove
from heat and stir in 2 cups of sprouted lentils or
sprouted mung beans or 1 cup of each—add ½cup of
minced parsley. Makes 4 to 6 servings.

WHEAT SPROUT CEREAL

Sprout wheat for 2 or 3 days. Now it is ready to use
fresh or to dry and place in sealed bottles. Before bottling you may want to crack the wheat.

To use the fresh sprouts—just pour over boiling
water or hot milk and eat as a hot cereal. This way it is
really full of nutrients. Do not take too much as it is
chewy and a small bowl is really filling. This is a cereal
that will stay with you a long time. This is an excellent
way to start the day.

To cook dried sprouted wheat, whole or cooked,
place in pan and pour hot water over them, let wheat
soak up the water—add more water if necessary and
heat until tender.

I know a very prominent man who takes a small bag of sprouted wheat to work—he has them for lunch each day.

A very wise man—there is nothing better.

You may treat all grains alike: wheat, rye, oats, millet, triticale, barley and other grains. They all make excellent meals served plain or with milk. Some people soak them in fruit juice the last night of sprouting. This is a real treat for breakfast, warm or cold.

WHEAT SPROUT TREATS

After sprouting 3 days—soak fresh wheat sprouts in a mild solution of salt water for 2 hours—drain well and place in a pan with sides. Then put into an oven set at the lowest heat. Leave the door open just a crack to let the moisture out. Stir occasionally until completely dried. Place in a bowl and let the children nibble.

Another treat is to sprout your wheat. Let it partially dry—place a little vegetable oil in a pan—heat—add the wheat sprouts and stir or shake until they are golden brown and split open. Drain off oil on an absorbent paper —sprinkle with salt. Delicious.

SPROUTED SOY CHILI

¼ cup vegetable oil
1 large onion minced
1 large green pepper—cleaned and chopped
2 garlic cloves
2 cups soybeans sprouted
1 lb. of ground round
2 tsp. chili powder
4 ounce can of tomato sauce
½ cup of water
½ tsp. oregano
½ tsp. cummin
    salt to taste.

Saute the onions, green peppers and garlic in oil—add ground beef—stir and cook until the pink color is out of the meat—remove excess grease from pan—add tomato sauce and water—mix and add soybeans and seasonings. Simmer until beans are tender as you like them.

Soy is the world's most valuable bean, offering all the essential Amino acids needed by the body to synthesize protein. They contain twice as much calcuim and thiamin as other beans. When sprouted, they contain valuable amounts of vitamin C. They require no special handling and can be used just as you would any other bean.

SPROUTED SOY NUTS

Sprout soybeans for 2 days—or until sprout appears—no longer than ¼ inch.

Soak sprouts in a mild salt solution for 3 hours—drain water off—heat a small amount of oil in a fry pan and roll beans gently in oil. Place beans on a cookie sheet with sides in a oven at low heat. Slowly roast beans until dry. Stir occasionally—cool and store in sealed jars in a cool place for use when needed.

SPROUTED SOY NUTS FOR BAKING

Prepare the sprouts the same as for soy nuts, only do not add oil. Cook on cookie sheet or in a cake pan. These may be used in place of nuts when making cookies or cakes. A real treat chopped and mixed in a sprout salad.

Store them in a sealed jar in a cool place.

MUNG BEAN AND TUNA TREAT

2   cans (regular) tuna
1½ cups cooked dry rice
2   tsp. prepared mustard
¼   tsp. oregano
2   eggs
6   slices of tomato
1   can condensed cheddar cheese soup
¼   cup of milk
1   cup chopped mung bean sprouts

Flake tuna with a fork—add rice—mustard—oregano—onion and add egg—mix thoroughly. Add mung bean sprouts and mix lightly—form into 6 patties—place on a baking sheet. Bake about 10 minutes at 450 degrees.   Add tomato slices and bake for 5 minutes more. Serve with sauce made with cheddar chees soup. Makes six servings.

INDEX to RECIPES

INDEX to RECIPES

Recipes   123

—NOTES—

—NOTES—

ORDER BLANK

HAWKES PUBLISHING INC.
P.O. Box 15711
Salt Lake City, Utah 84115

SHIP TO:_____

_____

_____

SURVIVAL BOOKS:

____HOW TO BE PREPARED—Roland Page	2.95	
____HOW TO GROW GROCERIES FOR $100 YR.		
—Clifford Ridley	2.95	
____HOW TO SURVIVE WITH SPROUTING		
—Bruford Reynolds	2.00	
____THE HUNGRY JOURNEY—Gordon Allred	2.50	
____MAKE A TREAT WITH WHEAT		
—Hazel Richards	2.25	
____HOW TO LIVE THROUGH FAMINE		
—Dean L. Rasmussen	2.95	
____NONE DARE CALL IT CONSPIRACY		
—Gary Allen	1.00	

BOOKS BY CLEON SKOUSEN:

____NAKED CAPITALIST	2.00
____NAKED COMMUNIST	3.95

BOOKS BY JOHN D. HAWKES:

____NEW TESTAMENT DIGEST	2.00
____ART OF ACHIEVING SUCCESS	2.00
____KEYS TO SUCCESSFUL DATING (hard)	5.95
____ (softback)	2.95

BOOKS BY RICHARD L. EVANS:

____RICHARD EVANS' QUOTE BOOK (hard)	4.95
____ (Gift Box)	5.95
____THOUGHTS FOR 100 DAYS—Vol. I	3.50
____THOUGHTS FOR 100 DAYS—Vol. II	3.50
____THOUGHTS FOR 100 DAYS—Vol. III	3.50
____THOUGHTS FOR 100 DAYS—Vol. IV	3.50
____THOUGHTS FOR 100 DAYS—Vol. V	3.50

BOOKS BY HELEN ANDELIN:

____FASCINATING WOMANHOOD	5.95
____FASCINATING GIRL	6.95

—NOTES—